What People are Saying about
Hope Beyond Suicide

Dr. J. Gordon Henry, former Executive Vice President for Academic Affairs, Liberty University (VA) and President of Northeastern Bible College (NJ), served on the Licensure and Approval Advisory Board of the New Jersey Department of Higher Education and the Board of Directors of the New Jersey Association of Colleges and Universities, is author of numerous books, and President of J. Gordon Henry Ministries.

"Dr J. Bruce Sofia has written an extraordinary treatise that both answers questions and provides a level of solace for all of us who have faced the tragedy of suicide. Drawing from the crucible of his years as an effective pastor-teacher, he has written a piece on suicide that is likely to become a Christian classic."

Jhan Moskowitz, North American Director of Jews for Jesus, and platform speaker for Promise Keepers.

"Sofia has brought the heart of a pastor and mind of a theologian to this knotty question. He has pushed the issue back to the forefront of the evangelical world. Whatever your view on the issue [suicide] Sofia's book will add more to your understanding."

Rob Schenck, Missionary to top U.S. Government Officials, Washington, DC, and author of *Ten Words that will Change a Nation*.

"Hope Beyond Suicide guides us to answers informed by the skill of a biblical theologian and the compassion of a shepherd of souls. This book is a great resource for anyone who has lost someone to suicide, for counselors to those who might consider suicide, and for all who wish to grow in their understanding of the Good News of God's love."

Steve Bell, Executive Vice President, Willow Creek Association, and **Valerie Bell**, Author/Speaker. Authors of *Real Survivors: Finding Hope and Courage in Times of Crisis.*

"Hope Beyond Suicide is a healing resource for those dealing with the aftermath of or the angst of someone considering suicide."

C. Samuel Verghese, (MD, Ph D), Biofeedback Clinic & Nature's Hospital, Missionary Physician, and author of *Brain Power: How to Fine-Tune Your Brain Naturally.*

"Dr Sofia's book constitutes a noble effort at grappling with many of the difficult concepts germane to suicide. It is a must read."

Sara Copeland-White, wife of the late, legendary Hall of Famer, Reggie White #92.

"I am excited that this book will comfort and help those who need understanding on this subject. Having counseled hundreds of people and by personal experience, no one is exempt from this fragile suffering from within and beyond."

Robert Fountain, National Police Suicide Foundation Trainer, Board Certified Expert in Traumatic Stress, Academy of Certified Master Chaplains, and Senior Pastor of Calvary Chapel Miami Beach, FL.

"Truly filled with hope, this tool will prove a valuable resource to anyone seeking to comfort the survivors of the all too common tragedy of suicide."

Terry Clark, pioneer in Contemporary Christian Music and conversational worship; Christian songwriter and recording artist with Word, Maranatha!Music and CatalystPeople.com.

"My friend, Bruce Sofia, with compassion and scholarship, has comforted the hurting and answered those who weep while wiping away their tears by gently refocusing the broken hearted on the mode of life rather than the method of death."

Hope Beyond Suicide

by J. Bruce Sofia

Hope Beyond Suicide

Hope Beyond Suicide
ISBN: 978-1-936750-75-7
Copyright © 2011 by J. Bruce Sofia
Cover Art by Barbara Februar
Cover art, titled *Angel 1*, is created by Barbara Februar.

Published by
Yorkshire Publishing
9731 East 54th St.
Tulsa, OK 74146

Printed in Canada. All rights reserved under International Copyright Law. No part of this publication may be reproduced, stored in a retrieval system or transmitted to any form or by any means — electronic, mechanical, photocopying, recording, or otherwise — without prior written consent of the Author.

Some Scriptures are taken from the New American Standard Bible®, Copyright © 1960, 1962, 1963, 1968, 1971, 1972, 1973, 1975, 1977, 1995 by The Lockman Foundation Used by permission. (www.Lockman.org)

Some Scriptures are taken from the New King James Version. Copyright © 1979, 1980, 1982 by Thomas Nelson, Inc. Used by permission. All rights reserved.

Some Scriptures are taken from the Holy Bible, New International Version®. (NIV®) Copyright © 1973, 1978, 1984 by International Bible Society. Used by permission of Zondervan Publishing House. All rights reserved.

Some Scriptures are taken from the Holy Bible, New Living Translation, copyright © 1996. Used by permission of Tyndale House Publishers, Inc., Wheaton, Illinois 60189. All rights reserved.

Acknowledgments

O ut of all the portions of this book, this is the scariest. I know that's not the most professional sentence in the world, but it's true, for me at least. How do I acknowledge those who have contributed to this book without in some way or another leaving someone out? My whole life is, as Bill Hybels would say about coming to Christ, "A series of inputs" – from my wonderful and privileged Christian heritage to the parishioner who would consider him/herself an average Joe/Jane, to teachers (elementary through post-graduate), to friends who have no agenda other than just being friends. Then, there are those who do have an agendum, and God uses them equally, maybe even more so, to shape my/our lives.

While working on my bachelor's degree in Art Education at Appalachian State University, I recall a professor saying, "We've had about every kind of person you can imagine come through this department, but you're the first Christian." Now, I wasn't the first Christian, guaranteed, but to him I was the first 'outspoken' and 'confronting' Christian. Most of my work dealt with religious themes and contained images of Christ. (This book contains one of them — a drawing we had to do from memory of a person we knew. I drew Jesus, who looked much like my father with the addition of hair and a beard.) All of these experiences are 'Acknowledgements' in my book.

But, the protocol for these kinds of things, I suppose, is to name specifically those who have contributed directly to *this* book. The progression is as follows. All the people who honestly shared their hearts when they lost a loved one to suicide: Rick Kern — thanks for being my second set of eyes, for believing in me as a writer and supporting me through this (and the next two writing projects: *When Divorce is Right! and Fornication -- The Lie that Drives our Times*). Jason Hannath — who found me when Rick and I were looking for a publisher (that's a story in itself); Jason's vision is far bigger than mine — I just want to write and bring healing to confused and shattered lives, he wants to rescue the dreams of every person on the planet whose life has been 'hijacked' by the tragedies and transgressions of life. I love Jason's zeal. And, Todd Rutherford — a friend of Jason's, who, after reading these book projects, believed that they were worthy of publication.

Now, let's get a little closer to home. 'Thanks' is a pale word to express my deep gratitude to the following people (those, too many to name, who have been true friends in a world where so many befriend for self-serving purposes — and that is the reality of life): the GCCC Advisory Board — which believed in and affirmed these projects with its support; Cheryl McFall — who has been my official proofer (spelling, grammar, things that don't make sense, etc.) both for my weekly sermons and these projects; Bethany Frye and Claudia Krusch — who have overseen the Spanish and Portugese translations of this project (and those who have worked with them); Woody and Evelyn Vanaman — who opened their summer home to me in the winter months so that I would have a place to write, free from distractions; a Pastoral staff and congregation that have pressed me for years to put the wisdom gleaned over three decades of ministry in a book; Geri Summerville — who put the heart of this book in three words, hence its title: *Hope Beyond Suicide*; my family — who has been in my corner through thick and thin, especially my lovely wife, Sheryl, who is my best friend and the greatest gift I've ever received, other than salvation.

Last and most important, a Heavenly Father who has loved me more than life itself, *literally*, who has not brought me to shame when so often I have repeated the same, as the modern day psalmist Terry Clark would put it, 'stupid thing.' LORD, how can I express my thanks for Your mercies, which are 'new' **every** morning? There are no words to do so — forgive me! To my Lord and Savior Jesus Christ, to a life-imparting Spirit — thanks, thanks, thanks. You do make all things work for the good of those who love You, including me.

J. Bruce Sofia

Preface

Pastor Chuck Smith, founder of the Calvary Chapel churches, once quoted a fascinating study done with Norwegian wharf rats that, believe it or not, demonstrated the power of hope. A group of these enormous rats was placed in a large glass chamber, half-filled with water. They gave up and perished in a mere 17 minutes! A second group was also put in the same chamber *but rescued just before drowning.* That second group was once again placed in the chamber half-filled with water but lasted *an incredible 36 hours —* Why? Because they had the hope of being rescued.[1]

Similarly, noted author Hal Lindsey wrote in his blockbuster book, *The Terminal Generation,* that "Man can live about 40 days without food, about 3 days without water, about 8 minutes without air, but only about 1 second without **'hope'.**"[2] Frankly, that has been my experience with what has been dubbed, 'the human condition.' People *will* find hope somewhere, even in a lie, even in death, because they cannot live without it! In fact, I have watched from a ringside seat many times as those I love deeply and dearly careen off

---

[1] Smith, Chuck. *'1 Peter 1:3b,' Chuck Smith — Sermon Notes. Blue Letter Bible.* 7 Apr 2005. 19 April 2011.
http://www.blueletterbible.org/commentaries/Chuck_Smith/sn/sermon.
cfm?SermonID=1.

[2] Lindsey, Hal. *The Terminal Generation.* (Old Tappan, New Jersey: Fleming H. Revell Company, 1976).

the rails and invest their heart and soul in what is clearly false hope rather than face a reality that *appears* to offer no hope. It is tough to grasp why people become so desperate for hope that they actually find it in death, believing that the blessing of life has become a curse. The reasons must be as diverse and unique as the people and their backgrounds.

There is no shortage of reasons to lose hope — it almost seems life is *designed* to leave the soul empty and aching at times. We all find ourselves gritting our teeth and holding our breath as we take hit after hit from the world around us. And yet, sometimes, the problem isn't really the problem — it's our attitude toward it that becomes toxic! I have known those who struggle desperately with the apparent inability, or even the stubborn refusal, to see life the way it is, insisting on seeing it the way they want it to be instead. It's a view that can't help but prompt a savage collision with reality and when that happens, reality wins. In extreme cases, it can lead to the unthinkable — suicide. It's not that people *want to die*, but that they *can't bear to live!* And this passion to look for hope somewhere other than life becomes so zealous and consuming, that it leads them to look for light in the deepest darkness.

However, contrary to the deception and the lies that people believe — hope is a constant. And though hurting people don't readily realize it, it is more common for them to abandon hope through believing lies about themselves and life, than hope abandoning them. From random acts of kindness to not-so-random outreaches of affection, support, and inspiration, hope lies in the details — never forget, it's the little things that often make the biggest differences. The late Dr. Glenn Martin, chair of the Political Science Department at Marion College in Indiana, used to drive a particular point home repeatedly in his renowned 'God in Government' lectures. He'd say something to the effect that *historically, even when outnumbered, outgunned, and out maneuvered, it was principally the person, army, or nation with the greater will that won the day.* It was as if their hope held the power to defy the odds, strengthening their resolve and giving them the edge — just as *our* hope has the same power.

Bruce Sofia has penned a set of books called the *Hijacked Life Series* to tackle the toughest, most controversial, and hottest topics. Writing with a shepherd's heart, he goes head-to-head with these issues having spent three-plus decades in the trenches with multitudes that have struggled through them. In this first volume, *Hope Beyond Suicide*, Dr. Sofia has examined the agonizing, bedrock problems that friends and family face when someone they love takes their life. What is the net-effect of their death? Where are they — Heaven or Hell? What is God's view of their decision, and has the hope they placed in death paid off? Have they finally found the peace of mind in dying that they couldn't find in living?

Dr. Sofia is more than qualified to speak into these and other critical questions related to the issue. As a pastor who has been officiating funeral services since entering the pastorate, he is much better acquainted, unfortunately, with suicide than he'd like to be. He has bathed this book in prayer while looking closely at a number of suicides, and contrasting his experience against the scriptural realities he has embraced during his tenure as a clergyman. In *Hope Beyond Suicide* you'll find the touching stories of people whose only hope was found in ending their life. You'll also find God's heart toward them, and a comforting, compassionate reassurance for those who have lost someone to suicide.

Through his unique gift for sharing God's love without compromising God's truth, Pastor Bruce has sketched a powerful, down to earth portrait of Heavenly principles — a portrait that is healing balm to those despairing from a friend or family member's self-inflicted wound. It binds the broken heart, nourishes the need for hope, and soothes the aching soul. It's been among my highest honors to play a small part in this project; I am greatly humbled. Without a doubt, I am a better man for knowing Bruce and I am confident that no one will be able to read this book and remain unchanged. I know — I will never be the same.

Rick Kern

Chapter One

she was just fourteen

I recall my very first funeral. The fragrance of flowers was overwhelming, and so was the event. The muted murmur of weeping echoed softly through the funeral home as tears flowed openly. New to the pastorate, I had to choke back my own; the scope of the tragedy was far beyond anything I had dealt with at this point in my life — and ministry.

She was new to the youth group, and just fourteen. Her future was bright, but its light was snuffed out, hijacked if you please by her hopelessness. She and her mother had gotten into a quarrel, what seemed to be one of many typical teenager/parent clashes — at least that was the word that had come back to me. The young teen told her mom they would never argue again. And they didn't. She went upstairs to her bedroom, a shot was heard. There would never be another argument — at least not in this life.

The fragile whispers of parents, classmates, and friends filled the room like fear filled their eyes, periodically giving way to an awkward silence as everyone struggled to know how to act and what to say. This was not a typical wake where people came to pay their respects, celebrate a life, and grieve a loss. This was different. A fourteen-year-old had her destiny and dreams hijacked by an immature, self-inflicted death. What fourteen-year-old could grasp the ramifications of such an act? That by taking her life she lost a life yet to be lived. With it begged the stifling question that hung in the air like the calm before a storm. A question everyone was asking but no one dared verbalize: She had committed suicide — where was she, in Heaven or Hell?

I couldn't help but wonder if she could have seen the implications of her actions, would she have still gone through with it? Adults who take their lives often are unable to see the consequences of their actions; what makes any of us think that a fourteen-year-old would understand them?

startling statistics

The *American Association for Suicidology* estimates that each suicide directly affects at least six other people — one in every 65 Americans[3]. In my book, that's too many hijacked lives and too many tears! Nonetheless, something else stands out in my mind about this teen's funeral, something more positive and inspiring — the 'word gifts.'

word gifts

Remember, this was the first funeral I had ever officiated. I was following the Methodist's handbook for the 'Order of Service.' I opened with a prayer; then read from the Old and New Testaments. Following the Scripture reading was the 'eulogy.' "How do I give this eulogy?" I asked myself. After all, I had only met this young teen one week ago. Instantly, I did what most of us do when we don't know what to do — I prayed. Immediately I sensed the Spirit say, "Open the floor for people to say a sentence or two. They know her. That's why they're here."

---

[3]   http://www.suicidepreventionlifeline.org/App_Files/Media/PDF/
PressRelease/Suicide%20PrevMonth% 20SAMHSA%20Press%20Release.pdf.

(*Rose Garden* by Barbara Februar – White Stone Gallery, Philadelphia, PA.)

What followed was absolutely beautiful: one by one, people of every age began to stand and give 'snap shots' of this teen's life. A sentence here, a paragraph there. A trembling voice, a trickling tear. A sobbing friend. In ten short minutes, those 'word gifts' helped me get to know a person I had only met once, and only briefly. Those precious moments had such profound impact upon my life. To this day, over 30 years later, I still open the floor for 'word gifts.'

mr. m

He was an upstanding man in his community, known and respected by all — a godly man loved by his family, friends, business associates, and church. Tragically, an operation that was a desperate attempt to correct Meniere's disease left his brain badly bruised. No one knew the extent of his suffering, but one day this man of upstanding reputation put a gun to his head and ended his life. The family found him in the bathroom with a pistol in his hand, his insurance policy, recently renewed, had matured the day before.

I can still picture the moment — a close friend who was a big guy standing over 6' 4" and rarely shaken by anything, fell back against the kitchen counter upon hearing of Mr. M's death, draped his face in his huge hands and gasped: "What a shame! It gives God a black eye." The world seemed to stop turning and screech to a grinding halt at the power of his words. "It gives God a black eye," he continued, clearly stunned. "It says God was not bigger than Mr. M's problem. So sad! So sad! So sad . . ."

Granted these are hard words, which some may consider judgmental, but that indeed is the tragedy of suicide. It takes a way out, which for many, at the moment, seems like the only way out — but instead it hijacks God's 'perfect' plan. And again, the life Mr. M had yet to live was not the only hijacked life in this tragedy — my friend, those who knew him, looked up to him, held him in high esteem; their lives were never the same. In fact, just yesterday, while driving by the home of the family of Mr. M, I thought how everyone's life was forever impacted, just as a part of our lives were hijacked as well.

mr. m's funeral

So here I was, still relatively young in my mid-thirties, and once again forced to answer the question raised by this family, friends, and associates — and the Church! Grasp this: whether you're watching a movie, listening to a religious radio program, or watching *Piers Morgan Tonight,* the question will arise with as many answers as there are settings for it — "Will a person who commits suicide go to Heaven?" Or maybe the question is better worded: "Will a person who commits suicide go to Hell?" — because that seems to be the dominating and overwhelming concern; no one wants a loved one to suffer eternal damnation.

As I again observed the questions gathering in the tear-filled eyes that passed by the casket, I heard the undercurrents: "Do you think Mr. M went to Heaven?" "I thought he was a godly man." "How could he take his life like that and be a Christian?"

Were there other unvoiced questions: Where else would he be — if not Heaven? And like the precious fourteen-year-old, the question was staring us all right in the face: Suicide — Heaven or Hell?

It matters not how well we know or don't know someone — it still hits us at the core to hear that a person has taken his/her own life. Every time I hear on the news, or at the Chapel doors (that's where I greet people after the end of each worship service), a story of suicide, I am reminded that suicide does not necessarily fit a preconceived profile. It can happen to people from any socioeconomic group, young and old, the state of mind hidden from even the best of counselors. Suicide, you might say, is no respecter of persons.

As for those of us left behind, we are abruptly faced with a barrage of emotions and questions that percolate through our minds, leaving us groping through the darkness for answers. For the immediate family and close friends, the sorrow is beyond comprehension. Suffocating waves of grief sweep over them. And just as the tears seem to dry, paralyzing emotional tsunamis hit with the mournful reality that someone they loved intentionally ended his/her life. This fourteen- year-old and Mr. M both took their lives for reasons family and friends may never fully understand. However, one thing is certain: something was wrong, something so deep that it left them utterly alone in their pain, unable to reach out for help.

(***The Bottom Line*** **by Barbara Februar – White Stone Gallery, Philadelphia, PA.)**

I can't help but wonder if that's exactly what you're doing right now while at a friend's house, on your couch, or in a bookstore with this book in your hand? Are you asking the same questions? Stay with me, the answer is coming.

My Journal

_____

_____

_____

_____

_____

_____

_____

_____

_____

_____

_____

_____

_____

_____

_____

_____

_____

_____

_____

_____

_____

_____

My Journal

_____

_____

_____

_____

_____

_____

_____

_____

_____

_____

_____

_____

_____

_____

_____

_____

_____

_____

_____

_____

Chapter Two

mr. d

He was bright with grand potential. Well-liked and popular, he could turn coal into diamonds and almost made you believe that alchemy was an exact social science. And money — goodness, his checkbook was bursting at the seams, *but* — (such a petite word with such a vast meaning — it seems to always revisit what precedes it) he had a drug problem he could not overcome! Every time it seemed he was on the top of his world, King of the Mountain, planting his flag on the summit of success — slam! Down he'd go until he was buried beneath an avalanche of white powder.

When he was on top, it was a grand slam across the board from romance to profession and everything in between — including his walk with the Lord. If he was in a drug rehab, he was assisting the dean within days. He fell deeply in love, married a wonderful young lady, and gave me the privilege of officiating what, by all appearances, was a fairy tale wedding. They had a bright, strikingly handsome son who began his life with a daddy who loved the Lord and was not afraid to tell others. But his gnawing addiction kept getting the best of him, and it was just a matter of time until he lost it all: marriage, job, friends, health . . .

I recall visiting him in a local rehab center where I couldn't help but think that even though falling that far was a sort of nightmare, there was something worse — refusing to wake up from it. Something Mr. D wouldn't do! He was on his way back up and doing fantastic — in fact, he could have run the rehab facility. Once he was released, again he marshaled his gifts and talents making remarkable strides in business, telling others about his faith, and attending church. Then it happened! He overdosed.

caution!

Now I say this with caution because I do not want anyone to think I am giving him/her license to take his/her own life. I address this matter because I have had far too many people who, after reading or discussing this truth on the subject, say: "Pastor, if I had heard this a year ago, I might not be here today. I may have taken my life." And, that may or may not be true; however, *truth is clearly truth* and must be stated as such. The 'doctrine of grace' is a great example of this. Scripture is unwavering on the subject: "For by grace you have been saved through faith; and that not of yourselves, it is the gift of God; not as a result of works, so that no one may boast" (Ephesians 2:8). This is what distinguishes Judeo-Christianity from all other faiths — you or I don't achieve a state of goodness/righteousness where God accepts us, but rather by receiving Christ, *His* righteousness is imputed (or applied) to us (2 Corinthians 5:21). It's not about us getting it right, it's about Him getting it right. Which He did! And He offers it to us freely at a great price (John 3:16; Romans 5:8).

In his first letter to the Corinthians, St. Paul tells these new believers that "Everything is permissible, but not everything is beneficial" (1 Corinthians 10:23). How can he say that? Because every sin — past, present, and future has been nailed to the Cross of Christ. Those sins, for us, were all future tense when Christ died. Now, let's go on record again: that does not mean there won't be consequences for wrong behavior while living on earth — what a man sows he reaps (Genesis 1:11; Galatians 6:7), e.g., Mr. D's death.

It was the consequence of sin. However, when it comes to one's eternal destiny and those transgressions being held against him/her, the Judge of all the earth rules 'not guilty' (Romans 8:1; Colossians 1:22). It is an eternal pardon.

Now, one could say that since all of his/her sins are paid for they'll just keep on sinning. But a true follower of Christ wouldn't deliberately keep on sinning (without a troubled conscience) because that would cheapen grace, God's eternal gift. St. Paul addresses this very subject in his letter to the Gentile church at Rome when he says, "What then? Shall we sin because we are not under law but under grace? By no means!" (Romans 6:15).

The point is this: just because "grace," also known as God's unmerited favor, covers all sin and therefore, unintentionally gives a believer the right to supplant what is right, it doesn't mean we don't preach and teach grace. Do we, as ministers of the Gospel, want people (believers or unbelievers) to sin? No, not at all! Sin messes *everyone* up! However, to preach anything other than grace would be an injustice to the gift of God; it compromises God's free and eternal gift. If man cheapens grace then he answers to God for that, but it doesn't mean we cease to preach the heart of the Gospel — which is truth and grace (John 1:14).

a great take on grace

By the way, here's a great illustration of grace. (I can't take credit for it; it was an illustration by one of our pastors while teaching the midweek service.) If I'm going at 20 mph over the speed limit and the police officer writes me up for 10 over, that's *mercy*. But if he doesn't write me up at all, that's *grace*. Grace is a complete pardon — an unmerited, free, and unearned gift.

a maxim to live by

Some time ago, the **Lord** gave me this maxim, which I have given as counsel more times than I can count: *Do right and give the consequences to God.* Addressing this subject of suicide 'head on' is doing right. What one does with this truth are the 'consequences,' and they must be entrusted to Him.

Sin is followed by grace, and grace is greater than all our sin as Romans 5:20b explains, — "But where sin increased, grace increased all the more." It's a merciful God that provides grace for our sin and it is also indescribably reassuring to know that God is as merciful as He is mighty.

Mr. D, try as he might, just couldn't defeat his demons. In fact, those who knew him had very high expectations of him and were certain that one day he would come out on top.

I wonder — if we could peer into our friends' and family members' lives from afar, would we be shocked to discover that they might be at a very weak or troubled point — possibly as vulnerable as Teen 14 or Mr. M or Mr. D? Is it not comforting to know that in their darkest hour, when they need it the most, and when those closest to them don't even realize how weak they may be — where sin increases, grace increases all the more?

My Journal

_____

_____

_____

_____

_____

_____

_____

_____

_____

_____

_____

_____

_____

_____

_____

_____

_____

_____

My Journal

_____

_____

_____

_____

_____

_____

_____

_____

_____

_____

_____

_____

_____

_____

_____

_____

_____

_____

_____

_____

_____

Chapter Three

the bottom line

H ere's the bottom line. Here's the answer to the 'Suicide — Heaven or Hell?' question. In geometry, it would be a postulate. In philosophy, it would be a proposition — I've framed with, 'if and then!' Here we go: If taking one's own life can send a person to Hell, then Christ's death is insufficient to cover *all* sin. If Christ's death does not cover *all* sin then no one is guaranteed eternal life, because salvation would then rest on us (man and/or the Church) and not in Him. It would be earned by us and not a 'free gift' (Romans 6:23; Romans 11:6). The only unpardonable sin, then, is rejecting Christ; that's yet another *Hijacked Life — Rescue Your Dream* hot topic.

Hebrews chapters 9 and *10* clearly state that, "Jesus died once for **all** sin," that includes suicide. Again, think it through! If suicide is all it takes to nullify the work of Christ on Calvary, then *no one* is guaranteed salvation and eternal life. Salvation would rest in us and not in Him. Andre` Crouch wrote, "The blood that Jesus shed for me will never lose its power." How true! For all who have trusted Christ, there is no stain of sin so deep that the blood of Jesus is not greater still. When we sit at the table in remembrance of our Lord's death, just before we drink from the cup, I'll often say: "We hold in our hands that which represents a detergent that knows no stain it can't remove." When it comes to salvation, *the way* in which a person dies is not the issue.

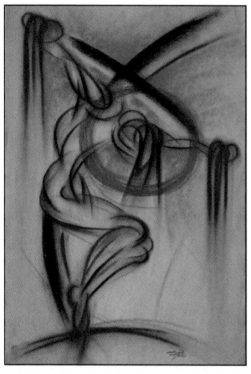

(*Christ on the Cross* by Tom Papadouplos – TAP Gallery, Williamstown, NJ.)

the promise of a forever with God

No passage in God's Word better addresses this matter of taking one's own life than **Romans 8:38-39**. Ponder these words:

"For I am convinced that neither death [any type, including suicide] nor life, neither angels nor demons, neither the present nor the future, nor any powers, neither height nor depth, nor anything else in all creation, will be able to separate us from the love of God that is in Christ Jesus our Lord."

As mentioned previously — to me, the shame and tragedy of suicide in the life of the believer is threefold: (1) the failure to see God as bigger than his/her circumstances, (2) the confusion and pain it leaves for loved ones, and (3) the hijacking of the dream blueprinted upon their lives by their Creator at conception. I suspect that the latter is the greatest tragedy.

this one puzzled everyone

Yet, I have officiated funeral services where the person who has taken his/her life seemed completely at peace with themselves and others. (I use the word 'seemed' because something was obviously masked to family and friends.)

for a bigger cause

We could discuss those who give their lives for a cause that transends themselves, such as Samson (Judges 16:30), men who lose their lives on the battlefield, yes and even the pilots who crashed their planes into the Twin Towers on 9-11. (I am not approving of what was done on 9-11, simply stating that they laid down their lives for a cause, which to them, transcended even their own lives.) However, that is not what we are looking at in this study. The pain for loved ones may be somewhat palatable in such cases as these, and our understanding satisfied. Whether we agree or disagree with the cause, when we get 'the why,' as unspeakable (or noble to some) as it may be, it brings at least a measure of comfort.

forever 18 . . .

I recall officiating a funeral for a beautiful young 18-year-old Hispanic girl who made everyone who knew her feel like they just won the lottery.

How vividly I remember her service — the church was packed. She must have had a special magic she cast over the young men she met; at one moment during the service I thought I was going to have to play referee for those who claimed her as the joy of their lives. I remember one fellow saying "I only met her once and for a brief moment, but I will never forget that moment; I have never felt so validated in my entire life."

She was a joy to be around. She excelled at whatever she attempted to do. She was not afraid to speak of her faith in Christ. She loved life and people. Her grave marker speaks of her effervescence — the placement of the marker in the cemetery, the color and shape of the stone, the place to put flowers, the words, the picture. Yet, one day, she abruptly ended her life here on earth.

Everyone who knew her, and there were no exceptions, could not figure this one out! It was truly a mystery. And now, forever 18, she is desperately missed by those who loved her, leaving them bleeding from a wound that will never completely heal. A wound from which more and more families are suffering, leaving in its wake gaping questions that cry for answers. Hijacked forever from our earthly existence is the joy she brought to all who made her acquaintance. It made no sense then; it makes no sense now.

St. Peter tells us, — "to every man an answer." I'm sure somewhere out there, or up there, is a reason why this beautiful 18-year-old took her life. But for now, we are all left wondering. Rabbi David J. Wolpe, in his book *Why Faith Matters*, after his wife was diagnosed with cancer and he lymphoma, wrote: "Suddenly, all that I had taught was tested in my own life. I understood that the essential question of life was not why does this happen, which we can never fully know, but how do we create something powerful and lasting from our wounds." Somewhere for 'forever 18,' she came to the conclusion that there was more value in finally wiping her tears away once and for all, than continuing to bring smiles to the faces of those whose lives she touched.

Her faith was real, vital, and dynamic — except when it came to believing in God's ability to heal one well concealed wound. I don't doubt that she was saved, or that God longed to bind her broken heart and save her from the tears she cried in secret. God has salvation for each of us all figured out, and it makes sense. There is a popular song that says, "Love could not be said a better way," referring to Jesus' death on the Cross, and ultimately God's plan of salvation. It's really true! There is no better way God could have expressed His love for us than to have died for us. Imagine how it hurts Him, after reaching to us through the Cross, to see one of His children destroy his/her own life and hijack His calling. It must absolutely break His heart, because God's children are precious to Him — in life and in death. The Psalmist wrote, "Precious in the sight of the **Lord** is the death of his saints" (Psalm 116:15).

I could be totally wrong. But as I assess this situation — and I am not a professional counselor, nor claim to be — this charming young lady, now forever 18, was hurting deeply, despite her successful efforts to hide the pain. Which, in a strange and incomprehensible way, showed that she cared — cared enough not to wish her burdens on anyone else. Whatever it was that she found unbearable drove her to remove herself from the situation, even at the cost of taking her own life. Something was terribly wrong — so wrong that she felt she would not be held accountable for what she did in desperation. For those left behind, that is the hope that they must cling to.

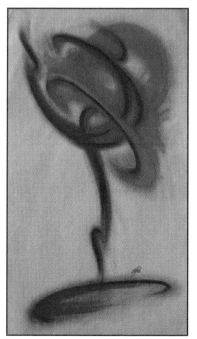

There is in us all something that wants to know the answers, to make sense of whatever it is that's out of order. And though we can live for a time without food or water, hope and faith are things no one can live without. An Old Testament wise man said, "Where there is no vision, the people perish" Proverbs 29:18a. What is vision but hope and faith? Faith and hope are what keep a person from giving up, from letting go, from checking out prematurely.

(*Ballerina* **by Tom Papadouplos – TAP Gallery, Williamstown, NJ.**)

My Journal

_____

_____

_____

_____

_____

_____

_____

_____

_____

_____

_____

_____

_____

_____

_____

_____

_____

_____

_____

_____

_____

_____

_____

My Journal

Chapter Four

i could not believe what i heard

I did not find it coincidental that one day during the writing of this manuscript, while listening to the radio in the car, a well-known pastor/evangelist was asked this very question: *Suicide: Heaven or Hell?* Unfortunately, the answer I heard was quite disappointing and, in my opinion, left the listener without any appreciable clarity. I am not being critical; each man/woman must speak from his/her heart with respect to knowledge of the Word. I'm just emphasizing the difficulty in getting direct and definitive answers to the question. However, regardless of the scenario surrounding one's death, the answer, according to my understanding of Scripture, remains the same. And, I believe it is anything but ambiguous.

for our answer

For our answer, let us go to creation's final authority for life, faith, and the practice thereof — God's Word, the Holy Scriptures. The Bible gives us six accounts of people taking their own lives:

- *King Saul,* after being wounded in battle took his life so that the enemy would not capture him alive.

- *King Saul's armor bearer,* upon seeing his master die in battle, fell on his own sword and died.

- *Ahithophel*, whose counsel was like the words of God, hanged himself when his advice was not followed by Absalom, King David's rebellious son.

- *King Zimri*, after seeing that the Capital City of Israel was taken by enemy troops, set his palace aflame and died in the fire.

- *Judas Iscariot,* hanged himself after betraying our Lord.

- *Samson,* who deliberately pushed down the supports holding up the grandstands of the arena he was in — the Philistines had brought Samson into the arena to make sport of him — and in so doing, ended his own life, taking three-thousand people with him in the process (Judges 16:27, 30).

First, let's establish the criteria used to answer the question, *Will a person who commits suicide go to Heaven?*

the criteria

Is the person a believer or non-believer? If the person commits suicide and is a non-believer, he or she will perish, not because of the nature of his/her death (suicide), but because that person did not trust Christ for the forgiveness of sins. John 3:36 says: "Whoever believes in the Son has eternal life, but whoever rejects the Son will not see life, for God's wrath remains on him."

For those of you who are saying, "Does that mean if a person does not 'receive Christ' he or she will not go to Heaven?" Yes, the Bible could not spell this out any clearer, that is why so many reject God's Word — it's too restrictive, too intolerant, too exclusive, too narrow.

A very famous, celebrated actor was recently interviewed (2009) on a popular TV show. He had been raised by his father, who was a Pentecostal minister (his mother left his father when he was an infant). This well-known celebrity was asked about his faith and what he believed. In essence he said that personally he could not accept Christianity because it was too restrictive. And he is right, it is. But that's what sets truth apart — it *is* restrictive, otherwise it would not be truth. When God set the Earth on its axis and determined its longitude and latitude, He created its seasons and a host of other critical details in relationship to the angle of the axis. That's empirical truth! You could argue that the pitch of our axis is restrictive because it cannot deviate even a little — but that is why planet Earth can support life. One degree off either way and we'd either fry or freeze — to death. Truth cannot compromise; that's why it's truth. Jesus said, "I am the way the truth and the life" (John 14:6).

At this juncture some of you are considering setting this little book down because what I've just said doesn't fit into your belief system. May I encourage you not to do so — this book may be small, but it has a huge message that could make a difference in your life and the lives of those whom you love — forever. Keep reading! God is **not** unfair and what may seem that way is almost always qualified by the 'but' which I will go into shortly — stay with me. You won't be disappointed; the 'but' is next.

the 'but'

But (this is one of my favorite subjects) — and that is one **big** 'but.' You have to love the 'buts' in the Bible. Here's why: the 'but' either negates what went before it or redefines it. For instance: "The wages of sin is death, **but** the free gift of God is eternal life through Jesus Christ our Lord." (Romans 6:23). In this case it negates 'the wages of sin,' how cool is that? Well, that's another topic in our

Hijacked Life — Rescue Your Dream series. Still, be aware that no one will ever be able to point a finger at the Father on Judgment Day and say: "You did not give me an opportunity to receive your Son!" However, like I said, that's another topic for another time. (If you'd like a head start on the subject, consider reading 1 Peter 3: 18-22, it will give you some fascinating insights into why no one will be able to point a finger at God and say, "You never gave me a chance!") Oh, one more thought on Judgment Day: There is a camp of believers who are touting that this will happen on May 21, 2011. If that is true this book will not come to print. If however, Judgment Day is not May 21, 2011, which is my persuasion, then this book has come to print and you're reading it.

if you'd like to know

And, lest I be remiss, if you would like to know how to receive Christ for the forgiveness of sins, go to Chapter Six in this book and read the portion titled, "Do You Know Your ABCs?"

My Journal

_____

_____

_____

_____

_____

_____

_____

_____

_____

_____

_____

_____

_____

_____

_____

_____

_____

_____

_____

_____

My Journal

My Journal

_____

_____

_____

_____

_____

_____

_____

_____

_____

_____

_____

_____

_____

_____

_____

_____

_____

_____

_____

_____

_____

_____

_____

_____

_____

_____

_____

_____

_____

Chapter Five

our purpose for living

As believers, our purpose for living is Christ (Philippians 1:21). Hence, when a Christian takes his/her life, it does not speak accurately of the God who can see His children through *anything* life brings their way (The promise of Philippians 4:13).

When a person stands upon God's promises, then suicide does not become an option, regardless of how difficult and despairing life may appear, because that person learns to trust a God that specializes in the impossible.

1 John 4:4 assures us of the power we have in the resurrected Christ:

> "You are of God, little children, and have overcome them, because He who is in you is greater than he who is in the world." (1 John 4:4)

> "I can do all things through Christ who strengthens me." (Philippians 4:13)

Furthermore, as we have stated numerous times throughout this book, when a person commits suicide the purpose for which that person was created is snuffed out — it is hijacked. Jeremiah 1:5 tells us: "Before I formed you in the womb I knew you, before you were born I set you apart; I appointed you as a prophet to the nations."

And Jeremiah 29:11 further confirms this truth when the **Lord** tells the Israelite exiles: "For I know the plans I have for you," declares the **Lord**, "plans to prosper you and not to harm you, plans to give you hope and a future" (Jeremiah 29:11).

We are not a product of random selection and chance; the Creator made us with a divine purpose, and *every* man, woman, boy, and girl has value and purpose, regardless of color or race, or where they're layered in the economic strata of society. Lest we forget, man was created in the image of God (Genesis 1:27). And though it's clear that the net effect of suicide hijacks our dreams and destinies on earth — the question still looms for many. There is no soft place to land on this one, it's right in our faces, up-close-and-personal again: *Suicide: Heaven or Hell?*

love ludlow

The question reminds me of a movie I saw called "Love Ludlow." I caught it on TV one evening while chilling out after a long, hard day. It told the story of Ludlow, a deeply-troubled young man who had been under the care of his sister, Myra, ever since their mother passed away five years earlier. On this particular occasion they were visiting their mother's grave, and while passing through the cemetery Ludlow asked Myra, "Will a person who commits suicide go to Heaven?" She responded by saying she didn't know (*Love Ludlow*. New York: Washington Square Films, 2005).

Interesting isn't it, that a troubled young man getting raked over the coals by life, would pose the same question asked by those who seem to have it all together, comfortably perched at the top of the food chain. To be quite honest, it was this question, "Will a person who commits suicide go to Heaven?" that I first heard over 30 years ago, and continue to hear today, even more frequently, that gave birth to this book.

(*Lazarus* by Barbara Februar – White Stone Gallery, Philadelphia, PA.)

does suicide send a believer to Hell?

So, does it? If a person takes his/her life, does it buy him/her a one-way ticket to Hell? Is it the end of the road? Does it extinguish all hope? *No!* God sees from a different perspective than we do. He has a worldview that is not of this world — it is eternal, while ours is bound by time. His ways are not ours. Life is not only about us, there is a Kingdom perspective that we may never understand until we see it from Heaven's streets. Therefore, let God decide when it is time to 'cross over Jordan' and enter Glory. In so doing, we spare so many whom we have come to love, and who have come to love us, much sorrow, questioning, and heartache.

Should suicide be an option for a believer? I would like to answer this with an unequivocal, explicit, "**No!**" But, to be fair, I have never walked in the shoes of a person who has committed suicide — therefore I will not be his/her judge. I don't know the pain that, in so many cases, has brought a person to the point in life where he/she feels that 'checking out' is better than staying — whether for him/her or those with whom they live. However, I believe I do have the mind of God when I say this: God has a plan for every believer that should be lived out to completion. When someone commits suicide, he/she shortens that completeness. All the potential for good, all the opportunities to bless and be blessed are forever gone. Romans 14:8 tells us:

"If we live, we live to the Lord; and if we die, we die to the Lord. So, whether we live or die, we belong to the Lord."

the picture is bigger than 'me'

May we always keep this truth in our sights — when circumstances don't make sense, when the pain seems too much to bear, the picture is always bigger than 'me.' Did Joseph understand his brothers' betrayal? Did Job understand his hour of trial? Did Naomi understand her misery? Did Daniel understand his captivity? Did Joseph understand Mary's pregnancy? Did Paul understand his imprisonment? Did John understand his banishment to the Isle of Patmos? Did that precious fourteen-year-old girl understand the value of a heartbeat, the privilege of touching and treasuring another's destiny, the priceless gift of making someone feel loved — feel that they mean something?

And though the fragrance of the flowers was Heavenly, back then at her funeral service, the question, *Will a person who commits suicide go to Heaven?* was Hellish and everyone was silently screaming it — just as they do today. To be honest, I did not answer it then because at the time I did not know the answer. Today I do.

However, this I do recall: I did not put her in Heaven and I did not put her in Hell. In Mr. D's case it was a sin unto death, which the Bible explains as a sin that takes one's life but doesn't damn his/her soul (I Corinthians 5:5; 1 John 5:16).

Some argued, "How can a person who overdoses go to Heaven?" The same way a person who tells a white lie goes to Heaven. The same way the repentant thief on the Cross went to Heaven. He or she is forgiven. Romans 8:1 is clear: "Therefore now is there no condemnation to those who are in Christ Jesus." The Death Row file is stamped 'PARDONED.'

degrees of sin — 'you betcha'

Now, as to the temporal world in which we live: are there degrees of sin with more far-reaching consequences than others? As they say in Montana, "You betcha!" Life makes few exceptions to this governing rule and I suspect when we stand before our Creator on Judgment Day, there will be no exceptions because, "what a person sows they reap" (Genesis 1; Galatians 6:7-8).

There are consequences to the lifestyle one lives. The popular word today is 'Karma,' while one of the age-old expressions is, "What goes around comes around." The biblical language is *what a person sows they reap,* or in today's terms, what you plant is what's you'll harvest (Galatians 6:7). However, when it comes to eternity, those who are pardoned are pardoned, period! They have **no** sin held against them (Colossians 1:22).

mr. d's funeral

Because of this I had no reservations placing Mr. D in Heaven when officiating his funeral. St. Paul said, "For to me to live is Christ, for me to die is gain" (Philippians 1:21). In Mr. D's case though, we lost; Heaven and he gained. The community, friends, and family lost because he believed the lie that he just couldn't win this drug-battle. Today, in the presence of the King, he doesn't experience defeat, but lives in victory.

judas

In clarifying this by way of contrast, Judas faced God as Judge, rather than Savior, and is probably is in Hell (in this author's opinion) because he rejected Christ as Messiah, *not* because of the way he died. Therefore, in addressing this question — we do so from the perspective that the person who takes his/her life is a believer. Again, here is the truth about suicide — it hijacks one's dream; it robs everyone of that person's potential, contribution to society, and the impact on the Kingdom of God. The act of suicide cannot be undone this side of the Jordan. All of his/her potential, promise, and remarkable possibilities are gone — never to be recaptured.

Let's explore this matter further. Imagine what would have happened if Judas had repented instead of hanging himself. Think about if Judas had not taken his life. Consider, for a minute, what it would have been like if, when Jesus, after His resurrection, had been met by a Judas who fell at His feet and wept, "Lord, forgive me for betraying you." (Hey, we're all there; our sin betrays Christ daily.) "I really do believe You are the Messiah. May I still be Your disciple?" Do you believe for a moment that Jesus would have denied Judas' request? **Never**! Never! Never! That's why He came: to seek and save those who were lost (Luke 10:19). That's you, me — and Judas.

In fact, I doubt Judas would have had an equal. I believe he would have been the greatest New Testament evangelist of the fourteen (including Matthias and Paul). But instead, an unrepentant Judas, who snuffed out his calling (remember he was a disciple) went to his grave *un*forgiven (Mark 14:21).

My Journal

_____

_____

_____

_____

_____

_____

_____

_____

_____

_____

_____

_____

_____

_____

_____

_____

_____

_____

_____

_____

My Journal

My Journal

_____

_____

_____

_____

_____

_____

_____

_____

_____

_____

_____

_____

_____

_____

_____

_____

_____

_____

_____

_____

_____

_____

Chapter Six

encounter with an atheist

I recall sitting in a courtroom in Woodbury, NJ, embroiled in one of those rare encounters with an atheist that only God can orchestrate. I kept my cool, maintaining a godly attitude although he mocked 'my' religion as believing in 'magic.' As I pressed him, hoping he'd admit to having done something wrong, he stayed a step ahead of me, knowing exactly where I was going. "By whose standard? Certainty not the f-ing Ten Commandments," he countered with a satisfied look. The courtroom grew as still as a cemetery, every eye riveted on me, shocked by Mr. S' use of the 'f' word, and wondering where in the world I would find a rejoinder equal to his. The perfect response came straight from Heaven. "Mr. S," I answered calmly, "use your own standard. Have you ever done anything wrong?" The slightest grin forced its way to the corners of his mouth as he unhesitantly admitted he had. "That's why there's a Jesus," I replied. To my surprise, he handed me his business card and said, "Someday, I might just visit your church."

do you know your ABCs?

The place to begin in knowing God is by receiving Jesus as your personal **Lord** and Savior for the forgiveness of sins. God doesn't make knowing Him difficult; He truly desires a relationship with every man/woman He created in His own image. However,

(*ABC's* by Tom Papadouplos – TAP Gallery, Williamstown, NJ.)

sin separates us from Him because He is holy, and we are sinners. Ouch! I know that's tough to take, but it's true. *James 4:17* tells us: "Anyone, then, who knows the good he ought to do and doesn't do it, sins." There is *no one* who escapes that definition, no one.

Therefore, God in His love provides a way in which the chasm of sin can be removed and a bridge to reconciliation restored. I have said for years: "It's as simple as ABC." Here it is:

Admit – your sins have separated you from God. (Psalms 14:1-3; Romans 3: 23);

Believe – that God did something about your sins through Christ. (The Messiah and final Pascal Lamb.) (Leviticus 17:10; Hebrews 9: 19-22);

Commit – yourself to being a follower of Christ (disciple) by trusting His righteousness and confessing Jesus as Lord and Savior. (Isaiah 53:5; Colossians 1:22);

Do it today! – We are not promised tomorrow. (Isaiah 49:8; 2 Corinthians 6:2).

If these four confessions make sense to you, then you're ready to take the next step and enter into the joy of salvation now. Say this simple prayer in which you commit to giving your life to Christ and receiving Him as your personal Lord and Savior:

Father in Heaven, I'm sorry for the things I've done that are wrong; I confess to you that I am a sinner; forgive me. Thank you for loving me and sending your Son, Jesus, to pay the penalty for my sin. Holy Spirit, come into my heart; Jesus, be my Lord and Savior. I give you my life. Amen!

welcome to God's family

For you who just prayed, welcome to the greatest family in the universe. And it's eternal. How cool is that? Rest in these words of our Lord: "[to] as many as received Him, to them He gave the right to become children of God, even to those who believe in His name." John 1:12 (NASB)

rest in this promise

Romans 10:9-10 promises — "that if you confess with your mouth Jesus is Lord, and believe in your heart that God raised Him from the dead, you will be saved; for with the heart a person believes, resulting in righteousness, and with the mouth he confesses, resulting in salvation." And that's what you've just done. So, trust in His promise; you are now a child of God and a citizen of Heaven.

what's next?

Tell me of your decision. There is nothing more thrilling than to know that a person has passed from death unto life: "The wages of sin is death, but the free gift of God is eternal life through Jesus Christ our Lord." (Romans 6:33)

I would love to hear from you. Write, e-mail or call me today. Don't wait! You'll look back and say, "I meant to" — Share your joy *now*!

E-mail: bruce@hijackedlife.com
Mailing address: 359 Chapel Hts. Rd, Sewell, NJ 08080
Telephone: 1-800-CHANGED

My Journal

My Journal

_____

_____

_____

_____

_____

_____

_____

_____

_____

_____

_____

_____

_____

_____

_____

_____

_____

_____

_____

_____

_____

_____

My Journal

_____

_____

_____

_____

_____

_____

_____

_____

_____

_____

_____

_____

_____

_____

_____

_____

_____

_____

_____

_____

_____

_____

Chapter Seven

why this book?

The World Health Organization (WHO) warns that suicide is among the three leading causes of death among 15-44 year olds; it is simply out of control across the board. From teens to the elderly, the alarming numbers continue to climb for a frightening variety of reasons that mental health professionals struggle to sort through. In the past four and a half decades, suicide rates have climbed 60%, and according to additional statistics provided on WHO's web page, a person attempts suicide every 40 seconds and one out of every 20 attempts is successful.

As it is easy to see on the WHO's global map, this blight is not just unique to America. The problem has grown so severe on a global level, that the World Health Organization has declared each September 20th as 'World Suicide Prevention Day.' In an effort to raise awareness and promote both commitment and action to prevent suicides across the world, the WHO and other partners advocate for the prevention of suicidal behavior, provision of adequate treatment, and follow-up care for people who have attempted suicide. In addition, the group encourages responsible reporting of suicides and coverage of the topic in the media.[4]

Almost weekly, I hear from someone who has lost a friend or loved one to suicide. For those left behind, the confusion and heartbreak are as relentless as comfort is fleeting, and the hope of closure, naive. Rick Kern, a former journalist and friend, writes:

"Suicide leaves behind a host of victims crippled by sorrow, drowning in tears, and crushed by questions. Where do they turn? And what can those who care about them do?"

(*Healing of Jarius' Daughter* by **Barbara Februar – White Stone Gallery, Philadelphia, PA**)

This book, the first in a collection of tactile gift-books, carefully confronting a number of critical issues such as this one, suicide, called the *Hijacked Life Series*, has been written to comfort the hurting and to answer those who weep while wiping away their tears.

As mentioned earlier in this book, push came to shove when, while listening to the radio, a well-know evangelist was unable (at least to my suiting) to answer the question: "Will a person who commits suicide go to Heaven?" I, too, remember when I couldn't answer that question. But I also remember when the **Lord** gave me the answer. It wasn't obscure; it is clearly in the Book. This book, *Hope Beyond Suicide,* has been written so that the moms, dads, grandparents, cousins, nieces and nephews, friends, and acquaintances who have lost loved ones to suicide can know that 'the act of taking one's life' cannot undo the forgiveness of Christ upon the Cross for all who have entered in. Romans 8:37-39 assures us:

". . . in all these things we are more than conquerors through him who loved us. For I am convinced that neither death nor life, neither angels nor demons, neither the present nor the future, nor any powers, neither height nor depth, nor anything else in all creation, will be able to separate us from the love of God that is in Christ Jesus our Lord. **Nothing can separate us from the love of God that is in Christ Jesus our Lord**. (*Author's emphasis.)

the hijacked life series

This book, along with its companion volumes in the *Hijacked Life Series*, has been born in the crucible of this pastor's life. The penetrating collection eclipses the 'Dear Abby' format by taking real life stories, struggles, and questions, and demonstrating the power of God's Word to surmount the unrelenting trials common to the human experience.

Someone may ask, "What qualifies you (that's me) to write these books?" Good question! My answer is not lengthy, but simply this: Humbly, may I submit, it is a combination of experience in the trenches as a Christian leader dealing hands-on with everyday-life issues, academic achievement driven by an inquiring mind, the pursuit of excellence, and a deep realistic love relationship with God that is never quenched.

Like my parishioners, whom I love and appreciate dearly, I am a sinner saved by grace who has wrestled with many of the same questions raised by the *Hijacked Life* series. As with you the reader, they have caused me to dig out the spiritual answers found in God's Word that work in the day-to-day grind where true worship meets the road. What good is a religion that is impractical? The Bible was written so that the man of God would be made complete, able to face the triumphs and defeats of everyday life (2 Timothy 3:16).

(*Dive Deeper* by Barbara Februar – White Stone Gallery, Philadelphia, PA.)

Over and over again, I have watched as a person's life is hijacked by behaviors that are in opposition to what our Creator desires for us. Allow me to elaborate:

"We live in a society that is quickly becoming devoid of God as it disregards His Lordship and ignores His voice."

The worldview, particularly in western culture, is that God and religion are increasingly irrelevant to the way we want and should live our lives. (Statistics seem to bear out that 80% of my mother's generation [she's 91 as of this writing] attended Church, 50 percent of my generation attend Church, and less than 10 percent of my son's generation [he's 31 as of this writing] attend Church.) With that in mind, let me ask, where then do we turn for answers to questions such as, "What is God's take on sex? Why did He create it and should His view of intimacy mean anything to me? If I want my date to end with sex as dessert, why would He care? And what about a same-sex relationship? Does the Bible get behind or between people of like gender becoming romantically involved? If so, why or why not? Isn't a loving God understanding of all kinds of sincere love?"

When considering these and other issues that infuse controversy in our culture and lifestyles, it behooves us to see things from God's perspective — always keeping in mind that His ways aren't necessarily our ways; but they are **always** the best way.

For instance, are we redefining reality and giving 'new' diluted names to things that profoundly set the course of an individual's and nation's future? Does a child in the womb now become a choice in the name of freedom? After all, it is my life, so what if I feel ready for sex but not parenthood? And, if I want to divorce 'for another,' what is it to God or anyone else? Should I stay committed to a passionless, empty relationship in the name of a love I don't *feel* anymore? A love that was once vibrant and meaningful, but now seems dead and predictable? In fact, my spouse resembles a roommate more than a lover, so isn't that the same thing as — "till death do us part?" I feel light years apart even on those rare occasions when we're in each other's arms, so why listen to this quasi-romantic death rattle? These are just some of the moral issues facing our society today that we explore in the *Hijacked Life* books.

(*Head of Christ* by J. Bruce Sofia, author of Hope Beyond Suicide.)

Hence, as in the book of Judges, a good summary of our post-modern culture is, — "each man did what was right in his own eyes" (Judges 21:25). Hasn't the result of that philosophy and lifestyle spelled disaster to cultures and kingdoms across history's tear-stained pages? Can we find ourselves, and America, between the lines written there, or does life simply go on without consequences relational to a culture's life-style (behaviors)? Are there societies that have survived and remained dominant influences where rampant immorality has become the rule rather than the exception? Can we throw off outdated moral restraints and say, "Yes we shall in the name of freedom!" when the Bible says, "Thou shalt not!?" To put it another way, which way of life protects both the culture and the sanity of those living in it? We'll tackle these issues in other *Hijacked Life* books.

my prayer

I realize that I am but one voice in a very loud world of billions clamoring for your attention. Yet, I know that one voice, when it resonates in the hearts of others, can change a world for the better. It is my prayer that the words of this book will light a candle of hope in the hearts of all who read it, and in so doing, light the sky in such a way that all who look up will be forever changed.

Final Thought

"God wants us to move through [each] day with a quiet heart, an inward assurance that He is in control, a peaceful certainty that our lives are in His hands, a deep trust in His plan and purposes, and a thankful disposition toward all that He allows."
— *Roy Lessin*

As my mentor, Dr Eugene D. Huber, used to say at every graveside: "Rest in this truth — to the 'believer,' life and love are everlasting." Indeed, the best of all is that God is with us in life and in death, no matter what the manner of our death may be.

I believe this benediction in Jude's gospel sums it up best:

"Now to Him who is able to keep you from falling and to present you before His glorious presence without fault and with great joy — to the only God our Savior be glory, majesty, power and authority, through Jesus Christ our Lord, before all ages, now and forevermore! Amen." (Jude 1:24-25)

My Journal

_____

_____

_____

_____

_____

_____

_____

_____

_____

_____

_____

_____

_____

_____

_____

_____

_____

_____

_____

_____

_____

_____

_____

_____

_____

_____

My Journal

_____

_____

_____

_____

_____

_____

_____

_____

_____

_____

_____

_____

_____

_____

_____

_____

_____

_____

_____

_____

_____

_____

My Journal

_____

_____

_____

_____

_____

_____

_____

_____

_____

_____

_____

_____

_____

_____

_____

_____

_____

_____

_____

_____

_____

_____

_____

_____

Chapter Eight

you're not alone

Maybe you have seriously considered taking your life. Maybe you have actually attempted it. Perhaps you are related to someone or have a friend who has tried to commit suicide — sadly, they might have been successful. I want you to understand that even though you may feel isolated and alone, there are people who care, and they are as close to you as the telephone.

Whether it is you or someone you love, the wounding and sense of hopelessness associated with suicide are real — but so is the healing. Let me encourage you to take advantage of the support services available, and begin to work through the healing process. While there are scores of outstanding counseling agencies, I have included a few that I can refer with confidence. Over the years they have proven to be able to meet people at their point of need:

1. *Focus on the Family (FOF):* Established by Dr. James Dobson more than thirty years ago, FOF is among the most credible and highly-esteemed family oriented Christian organizations in the nation. They have a referral department capable of coordinating therapeutic services with caring counselors who have been thoroughly vetted and are highly recommended. Call 1-(800) A Family (232-6459) or visit: www.focusonthefamily.com/lifechallenges/articles/

consider_counseling.aspx to learn more about their resources and referral services.

2. *Meier Clinics:* One of the most trusted names in Christian counseling, the Meier Clinic network has brought healing and hope to countless people since the mid 1970s when they were created to develop the best Christian counseling services available. With counseling and support staff embracing a nondenominational, Christian perspective on healthcare, Meier Clinics integrate biblically-based, Christian beliefs with psychological principles to treat the whole person — emotionally, physically, and spiritually. Their professional, highly educated staff of psychiatrists, psychologists, social workers, family counselors, pastoral counselors, and other clinical staff are committed to providing each client with individualized care tailored to meet his/her individual needs. With locations throughout the nation, many of their clinics offer Outpatient, Intensive Outpatient, and Day Program services assuring a seamless continuum of care. Call 1-(888)-7CLINIC (888-725-4642), or visit their website www.meierclinics.org.

3. *Lighthouse Network:* is a non-profit ministry, which provides **Help** and **Direction** so that people may better navigate life and grow in their walk with God through a unique and proven set of services, which include:
   - *Free Helpline* to find addiction and mental health treatment services nationwide @ 877.562.2565 x-101.
   - *Special expertise* in Christian and residential addiction/ mental health options.
   - *Leading-edge resources* and workshops on internet, DVD, and in person for individuals, small groups, and churches - Teaching Godly Decision-Making skills via

practical Bible application techniques for victorious living. www.LighthouseNetwork.org.

- *Stepping Stones Daily Devotional:* free, brief, practical, and unique; e-mailed every morning.
- *Solomon's Portico* free devotional and blog for those who are under 25 years old and looking for help.
- *Customized Solutions/Programs/Instruction* so that you may achieve your God-given potential and begin to develop a personal relationship with God.

4. *The Youth Alliance:* With chapters in many states and throughout different parts of the world, this multifaceted, non-profit organization works with other community organizations to encourage, train, and equip young people, giving them the tools necessary to break the chains of poverty, addiction, psychological and spiritual underachievement. Countering the negative undertow so prevalent among the youth culture, *The Youth Alliance* cultivates a commitment to achievement and personal responsibility, while inspiring discovery through God-given talents. Their programs benefit individuals and their families, which in turn impact local communities and ultimately the world. For more information contact the South Jersey office at: 1 (888)-480-SJYA or visit www.SJYA.com or www.theyouthalliance.com.

5. *The National Suicide Prevention Lifeline:* Are you feeling desperate, alone, or hopeless? Call the *National Suicide Prevention Lifeline* at 1-800-273-TALK (8255), a free, 24-hour hotline available to anyone in suicidal crisis or emotional distress. Your call will be routed to the crisis center nearest to you. With over 140 centers nationwide, the free and confidential service allows you to call 24/7 and talk to a caring person about yourself, or someone you are concerned

about. Visit their web site at www.suicidepreventionlifeline. org to learn more.

6. *911:* Dialing 9-1-1 will link the caller to an emergency dispatch center in nearly all locations in the United States and Canada. Known as a Public Safety Answering Point (PSAP), the dispatch center is able to send emergency responders to the caller's location. Should you feel suicidal or someone you are close to has threatened to hurt himself or herself, do not hesitate to call 9-1-1.

Suicide is usually the last resort for those who feel there is no way out. My reading, observation, and research on this subject reveal that people contemplating suicide will often speak of the subject as a noble way to die — I had a college professor who often spoke of suicide as a noble way to die. One day, he did not show up for class. Three days later police found his house in order, his bills paid, and him sitting in his car in the garage with the windows down — dead. Some will personalize the situation, expressing to others their own desires to end their lives; addressing the misery they are presently in.

When we are privy to such a conversation, we cannot brush it off like dandruff on a collar, as if there was no veracity in what we've just heard. In fact, just the opposite is true. We cannot hesitate to intervene immediately. The life of a friend or family member or whomever — maybe someone tells you of his/her thoughts because it makes them feel better, yet because you are but an acquaintance, you'll take it nowhere — is far too precious to look the other way, ignore the warning signs and hope that what you've heard will soon pass.

There are no more regretful words than "If I had only known." It is far better to say, "You're welcome," when someone thanks us for being there in his or her darkest hour than to say, "I only wish —" Be proactive! As the old expression goes: "Better to be safe than sorry!"

My Journal

_____

_____

_____

_____

_____

_____

_____

_____

_____

_____

_____

_____

_____

_____

_____

_____

_____

_____

_____

_____

_____

My Journal

_____

_____

_____

_____

_____

_____

_____

_____

_____

_____

_____

_____

_____

_____

_____

_____

_____

_____

_____

_____

_____

_____

_____

My Journal

_____

_____

_____

_____

_____

_____

_____

_____

_____

_____

_____

_____

_____

_____

_____

_____

_____

_____

_____

_____

_____

_____